MW00366870

The Joy of Mindfulness

*Declutter Your Mind, Relieve Stress,
Increase Your Awareness, and
Reclaim Your Inner Peace*

Neil Francis

Table of Contents

Introduction

Understand Your Roommate

Have you ever shared a room with a room partner? If not, assume for a moment that you are sharing with someone.

What if your partner is too talkative, a person who loves to speak all the time. On the top of this, if he or she knows a lot about you because you have been together for a long time, he or she might keep on saying things like:

- You are not good enough for that singing competition, so you better not participate.
- Here are the reasons why your parents loved your siblings more than you.
- You should never trust anyone because people take you for granted and use you on occasion.
- You should sit home, relax, and watch TV; why trouble yourself early in the morning to go running in chilly winter.
- And etc. etc.

What if this chatter goes on every time you are with that partner? What if this chatterbox does not allow you to focus on what's important in life? What if you feel frustrated and depressed while listening to this guy or gal?

What would you do?

If you're sincere about your life, you will choose either of these options.

1. You'll probably kick the person out of your room.
2. Or you get out of the room yourself and move elsewhere.

What if you own the room?

In this case, you'll definitely make your partner get out, so you can live a life of peace.

Now, let me pull the curtains away.

Everyone has a roommate like this. Yes, your mind is your roommate, doing this chattering all the time.

In case you haven't noticed, you have a mental dialogue going on inside your head that never stops. It just keeps going and going. Have you ever wondered why it is talking in there? How does it decide what to say and when to say it? How much of what it says turns out to be true? How much of what it says is even important?

Basically, you're not alone inside your own body. There are two distinct aspects of your inner being. The first is inner you: the awareness, the witness, the center of your willful intention; and the other is what you watch. If you can watch anything, it clearly means it is other than you; it means there is someone who is the observer. But the problem is that the other part you watch never shuts up. If you could get rid of that part, even for a moment, you would experience a sense of peace and serenity out of this world.

The irony is that you let this unchecked, monkey mind wander around and keep talking nonsense all the time. You not only allow this roommate to prattle, but you follow his or her instructions and change your behavior and actions based on the advice of this chatterbox.

What do these thoughts lead to?

This endless thinking most often gives you different type of feelings like stress, anxiety,

4

depression, frustration, restlessness, worry, and the like. These feelings are due to your uncontrolled thinking, and below is what happens:

Uncontrolled thoughts – uncontrolled actions – directionless life.

No one wants a directionless life. No one wants their actions to be controlled by something else. In fact, no one wants to be controlled by thoughts.

But why does it keep happening? Why do most people spend their lives running around like headless chickens?

This is because you have forgotten the art of disengaging yourself from your mind.

This forgotten art is called "mindfulness". Why do we say forgotten? Because you were born mindful; and you were mindful in your early childhood. If you try to remember, you'll recall those moments when you were so immersed in the little things that your entire attention was on that very thing, and nothing could distract you.

This is stage they term as mindfulness. Basically, it is a state of active, open attention on the present. When you're mindful, you carefully observe your thoughts and feelings without judging them as good or bad. Instead of letting your life pass you by, mindfulness means living in the moment and awakening to your current experience, rather than dwelling on the past or anticipating the future.

Mindfulness is an art and a way of training the mind to remain in the present. The issue or activity at hand is the top priority, shoving other distracting thoughts or actions to the backseat.

"In today's rush we all think too much, seek too much, want too much and forget about the joy of just being." - Eckhart Tolle

Why this book?

This book is written not merely to explain the detailed theory of mindfulness, but it is an effort to remind you about the forgotten art of mindfulness. You'll be surprised to learn about the benefits of mindfulness on your general health, mental health and over all well-being, as proven by scientific research and evidence.

I'll give you a brief reference of the origination and spreading of mindfulness as a concept from east to west. Meanwhile, the key objective of the book is to present you with enough techniques to instill mindfulness in your life.

You will learn plenty of mindfulness techniques for yourself in everyday life including how to implement it in your work life as well. If you have children or somehow associated with children, you know very well that childhood is foundation of life; therefore, the book contains an entire chapter on using the mindfulness technique through games and other means.

Finally, let's admit that there are some people who, unfortunately, suffer a lot in life and are plagued with stress, anxiety, depression, etc. This book explains how mindfulness- based stress reduction and cognitive therapies can help you come out of those testing times and start living a life of peace and meaning.

Chapter 1: What is Mindfulness?

What is Mindfulness?

Mindfulness, in plain terms, is just being mindful of what is happening within you, i.e., the thoughts going on in your head, the emotions you are feeling, the sensations or vibrations you are experiencing in different parts of your body. Being mindful affords us the opportunity to be less judgmental and begin to be fully curious about how the mind works, making us kinder, more accommodating and more loving both to ourselves and to others.

As a characteristic, mindfulness **is not alien to us**. It is what we do, and how we are built, manifesting in many different nomenclatures. It **isn't a special ability**. Just the way, Newton didn't invent gravity, nor did the Buddha invent mindfulness, it's just that too many people are embroiled in distractions from the external environment and have become largely spur-of-the-moment beings, with little effort exerted to be in charge of one's mental state. But the good news is that it can be cultivated.

To master it, it does not necessarily mean we have to change who we are. It **is best to recognize who we are and work with what we have, with the aim of making the best of it**. And to add the icing on the cake, when we become mindful individuals, we would be shocked at how well and far we can re-invent ourselves and discover parts of us that were hidden or fallow. This is the power of the human mind.

Mindfulness is not a faith thing. It is evidential and its rewards speak for themselves. Generally, it is something that should be encouraged, taught and practiced. "Mindfulness" is something you possess but you probably do not practice it because of the everyday buzz you encounter in your surroundings. It is a concept we likely have heard of, but don't put much effort into understanding it because we feel we need less of it.

In fact, mindfulness is the thrust of many meditative programs like yoga, which helps to declutter the mind and cause it to focus. It is the ability of the individual to be fully aware of where he or she is, as well as what he or she is doing, and what he or she aims to achieve. It is an all-important virtue that everyone needs to possess: it is something that needs to be possessed rather than employed on impulse.

A Few Definitions

To put it simply, mindfulness is a state of active, open attention on the present. When you're mindful, you carefully observe your thoughts and feelings without judging them as good or bad. Instead of letting your life pass you by, mindfulness means living in the moment and awakening to your current experience, rather than dwelling on the past or anticipating the future.

Below are a few scholarly definitions of mindfulness to elaborate different aspects.

- Mindful Awareness Research Center at the University of California at Los Angeles defines mindfulness as maintaining a moment-by-moment awareness of our thoughts, feelings, bodily sensations, and the

surrounding environment, through a
gentle, nurturing lens.

- Mindfulness is the psychological
  process of bringing one's attention to
  the internal and external experiences
  occurring in the present moment,
  which can be developed through the
  practice of meditation and other
  training. (Wikipedia)

Jon Kabat-Zinn has come up with a succinct
definition of mindfulness which states:
"Mindfulness is awareness that arises
through paying attention, on purpose, in the
present moment, non-judgmentally."

Precisely, mindfulness is paying attention in
three particular ways: on purpose, in the
moment, and without judgment. You can
practice mindfulness of breathing, eating,
bodily sensations (body scan), thoughts,
emotions, communication (listening and
speaking) and walking or other activities.
With practice, you can become more
mindful throughout the day, not just during
formal practice periods. For example, you
can practice mindfulness by focusing
completely on drinking a hot cup of tea,

taking in its scent, warmth, and taste and removing overpowering emotions from the mind.

"The best way to capture moments is to pay attention. This is how we cultivate mindfulness." – Jon Kabat-Zinn

History of Mindfulness

The concept of mindfulness originates from Buddhism, Hinduism, Judaism, Christianity and Islam (Trousselard et al., 2014), but it is not necessarily a religious practice because anyone can do it. Below is a brief mention about how the mindfulness term was coined from two famous religions before it reached the US.

- **Hinduism**

Hinduism is widely practiced in the Indian subcontinent, also called the oldest religion in the world. It has many interwoven traditions best known for their spiritual practices, and meditation is one of them. The earliest writings about the practice of contemplation or Dhyana (meditation) come from the Vedic texts of India dating back to approximately 1500 BCE, which include yogic and meditation.

Meditation or Dhyana is an activity that helps clean the mental toxins; according to Bhagavad Gita, a Hindu scripture in Sanskrit, meditation deepens our understanding of skillful actions and smart choices as it teaches us to be wiser, happier and a better person. The below excerpt from the Bhagavad Gita signifies the pivotal role of mindfulness:

"The Mind is the friend of those who have control over it; mind acts like an enemy to those who do not have control on it; and meditation is the process of washing the mind by the mind so you have your thoughts under your control. "

- **Buddhism**

Do not dwell in the past; do not dream of the future, concentrate the mind on the present moment. - Buddha

Buddhism as a religion arose in the eastern part of Ancient India and is based on the teachings of Siddhārtha Gautama known as the Buddha, who was himself awakened (enlightened) at the age of 35. The religion boasts of about 300 million followers around the world and originated about 2,500 years ago; it has played a central role in the spiritual, cultural, and social life of Asia during the 20th century before it spread to the West.

In fact, Jon Kabat Zinn, who brought the concept of mindfulness to the US was a student of Buddhist teachers, such as Thich Nhat Hanh.

Arrival in the US

The arrival of Mindfulness in the US is attributed to Jon Kabat-Zinn, a Professor of Medicine, Emeritus, and creator of the Stress Reduction Clinic and the Center for Mindfulness in Medicine, Health Care, and Society at the University of Massachusetts Medical School. Kabat-Zinn was first introduced to the philosophy of Buddhism while a student at MIT. Later, in 1979, he founded the Stress Reduction Clinic at the University of Massachusetts Medical School, where he adapted Buddhist teachings on mindfulness, by combining them with medical research findings to develop the Stress Reduction Program.

Mindfulness, as it entered into the mainstream of western world, was primarily for a therapeutic purpose. In 1979, Jon Kabat-Zinn recruited chronically ill patients who were not responding well to traditional treatments to participate in his newly-formed eight-week mindfulness-based stress-reduction program to help them develop the ability to see their pain more objectively and learn how to relate to it differently to suffer less. This treatment based on the concept of mindfulness worked well and thus prompted many scholars and psychologists to come up with numerous definitions and research studies demonstrating how mindfulness-based interventions can help change our brains for the better.

The main goal of mindfulness is to wake up to the inner workings of our mental, emotional, and physical processes and fully experience life. Scientists and researchers have gone a long way to scientifically prove that mindfulness can indeed improve or reduce the part of the brain that keeps us in a stressful state, covered in the next chapter.

Characteristics of Mindfulness

"Meditation practice isn't about trying to throw ourselves away and become something better. It's about befriending who we are already." - **Pema Chödrön**

Once we understand that mindfulness is an experience, it's important to notice how and why we should develop a non-judgmental attitude toward it without using any belief systems or imposing rigid values on ourselves or others. Only if you become non-judgmental about practicing mindfulness, will it help you to reap the full benefits. To help you further clarify the concept of mindfulness, let's look at the key characteristics. According to Gunaratana (1996), there are several basic aspects of mindfulness:

1. Acceptance

If you are unable to accept yourself completely--your imperfections and perfections, your highs and lows, your good and bad--it will be difficult to observe yourself and your environment without being non-judgmental. You need to accept yourself so that you will be able to notice unpleasant or difficult thoughts, feelings, and sensations in order to take an active stance in acknowledging and managing them.

2. Nonjudgmental observation

You need to observe your own experience without getting caught up in assigning judgment to any of it. You also need to learn to cultivate an attitude that takes an active and curious interest in things precisely as they are, with no efforts to change or deny any of it. Through this balanced observation comes an increased awareness of intricacy that helps you to become an open minded and a curious observer.

3. Unbiased watchfulness

It is easier to view things "objectively" when reflecting on someone else; but when it comes to yourself, not so much, which is why it is easier to point fingers at someone else when something goes wrong. However, mindfulness allows us to become more in tune with our internal, observing-self and enables us view our thoughts and feelings with more clarity and openness.

4. Non-conceptual awareness

Through mindfulness, we have the opportunity to experience what it is like to observe all things as if for the very first time. It gives us a fresh perspective of things we are familiar with and those we are not. When there is no agenda, we do something without pressure and in a different light.

5. Present-moment awareness

Mindfulness is being involved in and aware of your present moment; it is observing and acknowledging everything around from your body, to the activities near you, to the color of the clouds. This is a way to snap out of the sense of being on "automatic pilot" that many people in fast-paced western society experience, and it is also the ability to notice your thoughts as they are happening.

What is the difference between Mindfulness and Meditation

Most people think that mindfulness and meditation are one and the same thing; while, in fact, they are two different things – though they are closely connected and supplement each other. Let's understand the difference.

While mindfulness means entirely focusing on the present moment, the key aspect here is that we can do it anywhere and anytime. It's noticing and paying attention to thoughts, feelings, behavior, and everything else. It can be practiced at any time, wherever we are, whoever we are with, and whatever we are doing, by showing up and being fully engaged in the here and now. Mindfulness is simple in its form; you just need to be feel your presence – you catch yourself and observe whatever is going on. Be present and don't worry about the future; don't mourn the past. If you are drinking tea, or eating food, or even exercising, you watch your thoughts, the sensations in the body, and that's it. You can complete one session of mindfulness while sipping your tea. That's the simplicity of mindfulness.

Now coming to meditation! This is setting time aside in a quiet place for a specific time on regular basis. Meditation is different from mindfulness in the sense that it moves you to a different level of thinking. Einstein once said that we can't solve our problems at the same level of consciousness or thinking as they were created; we need to raise our level of consciousness to solve problems. Meditation does the job of changing the level of thinking or consciousness. It's not simply focusing on the present moment and observing what's happening around us; rather, it's sitting specifically with a clear objective of enhancing our level of consciousness and focusing deeply within on "no-thing".

Although mindfulness is considered a form of meditation, there is a different way of practicing the two. Yet, despite these differences, you can very well say that both mindfulness and meditation are mirror-like reflections of each other. Mindfulness supports and enriches meditation, while meditation nurtures and expands mindfulness.

Chapter 2: Benefits of Mindfulness: What Science Says

As you know by now, mindfulness is the conscious effort you put in to be aware of your surroundings and activities at the current moment without judging. But you'd be surprised to notice that this simple act of staying in the present moment has so many benefits on human health. There is enough scientific research on the effect of mindfulness that proves beyond doubt that it impacts stress reduction and enhances happiness; it even changes the physical structure of your brain to improve cognitive ability.

In this chapter, we look at the overall benefits of mindfulness based on reviews of relevant scientific studies before we move on to learn the best ways to practice it in our everyday lives.

Scientific Research on Mindfulness

Sara Lazar, a neuroscientist at Harvard Medical School, used the MRI technology to look at very fine and detailed brain structures to observe the inner physical changes while a person is performing a certain task, including yoga and meditation.

In her first study[1], Lazar looked at individuals with extensive meditation experience, which involved focused attention on internal experiences (no mantras or chanting). The data proved, among other things, that meditation may slow down or prevent age-related thinning of the frontal cortex that otherwise contributes to the formation of memories. Common knowledge says that when people get older, they tend to forget stuff. Interestingly, Lazar and her team found out that 40–50-year-old meditators had the same amount of gray matter in their cortex as 20–30-year-old ones.

For her second study[2], she engaged people who had never meditated before and put them through a mindfulness-based stress reduction training program, where they

---

[1]

https://www.ncbi.nlm.nih.gov/pmc/articles/PMC1361002/

[2]

https://www.ncbi.nlm.nih.gov/pmc/articles/PMC3004979/

took a weekly class and were told to perform mindfulness exercises, including body scan, mindful yoga, and sitting meditation, every day for 30 to 40 minutes. Lazar wanted to test the participants for positive effects of mindfulness meditation on psychological well-being and alleviating symptoms of various disorders such as anxiety, depression, eating disorder, insomnia, or chronic pain.

After eight weeks, Lazar found out that the brain volume increased in many regions, including the hippocampus, the part responsible for learning, storage of memories, spatial orientation, and regulation of emotions; and the temporoparietal junction, the area where temporal and parietal lobes meet, responsible for empathy and compassion. On the other hand, the brain volume decreased in the amygdala, an almond-shaped structure responsible for triggering the fight-or-flight response as a reaction to a threat, whether real or perceived.

A 2012 UCLA study published in the journal Frontiers in Human Neuroscience has discovered that long-term meditators have larger amounts of gyrification, or folding of the brain's cortex, compared to people who don't meditate. Gyrification increases the surface area of the brain and enhances neural processing. This may imply that regular mindfulness practice can only lead to improvement in the way the brain processes information, makes decisions, forms memories, and so forth.

According to Black (2010), a meta-analytic review by Sawyer and Witt in 2010 found that mindfulness-based therapies have a dramatic effect on improving both depression and anxiety. Research is currently being conducted or has recently been completed on the effectiveness of mindfulness practices in youth. Willingham (2011) notes that teachers who use emotion regulation skills in their classrooms can improve the self-control capacities of their students.

Research has also shown that meditation practices can help with a variety of issues, including substance abuse, trauma, anxiety, and depression.

According to neuroscience research, mindfulness practices dampen activity in our amygdala and increase the connections between the amygdala and prefrontal cortex. Both these parts of the brain help us to be less reactive to stressors and recover better from stress when we experience it.

One research study found that premedical and medical students reported less anxiety and depressive symptoms amongst others after participating in an eight-week mindfulness-based stress reduction training compared with a waiting list control group (Shapiro et al., 1998).

Another study published in the Journal of Clinical Sports Psychology found that athletes who practice mindfulness meditation techniques are far more motivated to exercise regularly and are more satisfied with their workouts than less-mindful individuals.

According to some findings, the regular practice of mindfulness can rewire the circuitry of the brain and help you learn and remember things. Physical evidence obtained from MRI scans proves that regular practice of mindful meditation increases gray matter in the hippocampus. This part of your brain is associated with learning and memory powers. In other words, practicing mindfulness daily for at least 10-15 minutes can enhance the ability to learn and remember.

Practicing guided meditation and other relaxation exercises regularly for a long time results in an increased amount of active genes. These genes help the body fight serious diseases and disorders like autism, cancer, insomnia, etc.

Here is a list of the major benefits that mindfulness can have on your mental and general health, as proven by scientific studies and research.

1. It helps reduce stress and anxiety

It is mainly known that relaxation through mindfulness is the main element in reducing stress drastically because it facilitates an adaptive response to daily stressors and regulates emotions that lead to better moods. The amygdala portion of the brain is responsible for fight, flight or freeze responses; it is the fear center of our brain. Scientific studies have evidenced that the mindfulness has the impact of reducing the size of amygdala. It also reduces the level of cortisol (the stress hormones) in our brain and thus control.

The symptoms of stress include anxiety, depression, insomnia, high blood pressure, heart disease among others; and when you de-clutter your mind using the stress management technique, you find your body and mind calming down and connecting to your environment.

2. It helps you deal better with illness

A study of MBSR in Chinese breast cancer survivors provided evidence that mindfulness can enhance post-traumatic growth and decrease stress and anxiety in cancer patients (Zhang, Zhou, Feng, Fan, Zeng, & Wei, 2017).

3. It decreases depression

Mindfulness has long been considered an effective supplemental treatment for depression. It has been found to decrease depressive symptoms, anxiety, and stress in college students, as well as increasing self-compassion when compared with yoga alone (Falsafi, 2016).

Mindfulness helps to enhance practitioners' ability to regulate their emotions by identifying them and being able to accept them; this will help you cope better and manage situations and thoughts.

4. It boosts resilience

Mindfulness training has been shown to boost resilience in children and help them understand and regulate their emotions (Coholic, 2011; Coholic, Eys, & Lougheed, 2012). Mindfulness helps us deal with our daily struggles and develops us emotionally, psychologically, and academically as we gain valuable skills from the technique.

5. It helps increase focus

Mindfulness meditation practice and self-reported mindfulness are correlated directly with cognitive flexibility and attentional functioning (Moore and Malinowski, 2009). Mindfulness helps with the ability to focus attention and suppress distracting information, which will help in various areas like meetings, work performance, and academics. As backed by science, mindfulness improves the gray matter in the hippocampus area of the brain, which is responsible amongst other functions for learning more and better memory

6. It increases cognitive flexibility

Mindfulness makes us more self-aware and develops our self-observation skill, helping us respond to situations better. Meditation also activates the brain region associated with more adaptive responses to stressful or negative situations (Cahn & Polich, 2006; Davidson et al., 2003).

7. It improves Emotional Intelligence

Consistently watching your thoughts and emotions curtails your tendency to be reactive upon the arousal of emotions like anger or stress. Since you are the person witnessing the emotions, you can, therefore, can rationally decide whether a particular emotion is going to help you or make you repent later. Mindfulness practice helps you to develop Emotional Intelligence.

8. It improves relationships

The University of North Carolina at Chapel Hill conducted a study that showed there is a correlation between the successes of couples who have been practicing mindfulness. Couples who practice mindfulness demonstrate a deeper level of closeness; they are more accepting of each other; and they are just generally more satisfied. Mindfulness training has also been shown to help family relationships. Adults are happier with their parenting when practicing mindfulness; they are less stressed and more interactive.

After learning the benefits that mindfulness can bring to your life, it is a no-brainer to start implementing mindfulness in your life as soon as you can. The rest of this book is about implementing mindfulness practices in all areas of your life. We will start with preparatory steps in the next chapter.

Chapter 3: Are You Ready for Mindfulness?

Mindfulness training is a combination of meditation and body awareness exercises that can help you prepare for and recover from stressful situations. To practice mindfulness, you have to prepare the mind, soul, and body; and you have to be dedicated and consistent to be able to reach the desired result.

To prepare your mind, you need to be willing to learn new things by stepping out of the box and move out of your comfort zone. You also need to be willing to commit, as they say "no pain, no gain." Be willing to sacrifice your time to this effort as your desired result cannot come in a mere day.

To prepare your body, you need to be willing to experience your own body and do away with unpleasant foods you consume that may not be healthy. Eat a colorful meal in the sense that it has the nutrients you need for energy like the vitamins and protein. Exercise at least 3 times a week to strengthen the heart and mind. A simple exercise like taking the stairs instead of the elevator at work goes a long way. Also, shower at least twice a day--before and after work--to remain pleasant and calm the nerves.

To prepare your soul, you need to prepare your spirit to be more open and flexible, as mindfulness is the ability to understand and be aware of your surroundings.

Mindfulness Training is practicing some exercises to help you pay conscious attention to your body, mind, and environment at the present moment without judgment. The meditation part of training consists of exercises that can be practiced without a formal session; it can be slotted in anywhere you go like mini-breaks, where you stop everything you're doing and sit and notice the sensations around you-- walking meditation, yoga, tai- chi and the common breathing exercise.

How to Develop a Daily Mindfulness Meditation Routine

'

You practice mindfulness, on the one hand, to be calm and peaceful. On the other hand, as you practice mindfulness and live a life of peace, you inspire hope for a future of peace. - Thich Nhat Hanh

You need to prepare for mindfulness just as you would for other activities; think and plan beforehand to know your next step and how you want to go about it. This might seem random; but when you know the activities you want to do, you will make a conscious effort to do it and do it right. To make something part of your routine, the best thing is to do it daily. You can start meditation with as little as 10 minutes a day, and then increase it further. I found this article[3] relevant, which shows a step-by-step process to build your daily routine. Here are the steps:

1. **Routine place:** this can be wherever you can sit easily with minimal disturbance. The key requirement is to choose a place that is distraction free or with the least distractions. Arrange what is around so that you are reminded of

---

[3] https://www.mindful.org/developing-a-daily-practice/

your meditative purpose, and it feels like a peaceful space.

2. **Regular practice time** that suits your schedule and temperament. If you are a morning person, experiment with a sitting before breakfast. If evening fits your temperament or schedule better, try this first. Begin with sitting ten or twenty minutes at a time. Later you can sit longer or more frequently. Daily meditation becomes like bathing or tooth brushing. It can bring a regular cleansing and calming to your heart and mind.

3. **Find a posture** on a chair or cushion in which you can easily sit erect without being rigid. Let your body be firmly planted on the earth, your hands resting easily, your heart soft, your eyes closed gently. At first, feel your body and consciously soften any obvious tension. Let go of any habitual thoughts or plans.

4. **Feel the sensations of your breathing**. Take a few deep breaths to sense where you can feel the breath most easily, as coolness or tingling in the nostrils or throat, as movement of the

chest, or a rise and fall of the belly. Then let your breath be natural. Feel the sensations of your natural breathing very carefully, relaxing into each breath as you feel it, noticing how soft sensations come and go with the changing breath.

5. **Notice your minding wandering.** When you notice this, no matter how long or short a time you have been away, simply come back to the next breath. Before you return, you can mindfully acknowledge where you have gone with a soft word in the back of your mind, such as "thinking," "wandering," "hearing," "itching." After softly and silently naming to yourself where your attention has been, gently and directly return to feel the next breath. Later on in your meditation, you will be able to work mindfully with all the places to which your mind wanders; but for initial training, one word of acknowledgement and a simple return to breath is best.

6. **Let the breath change rhythms naturally**, allowing it to be short, long, fast, slow, rough, or easy. Calm yourself by relaxing into the breath. When your

breath becomes soft, let your attention become gentle and careful, as soft as the breath itself.

Simple Mindfulness Exercises

It is important and quite rewarding to take time to sit for mindfulness meditation on a regular basis. Regular practice of mindfulness exercises can calm our bodies, souls, and minds instead of our emotions staying in flight mode all the time influenced by negative past experiences and fears of future uncertainties. We harness the ability to root the mind in the present moment and deal with life's challenges in a clear-minded, calm, assertive way.

It's unfathomable that one doesn't have ten minutes a day to sit silently for meditation, but some people aren't able to convince themselves to do it. They think they don't even have time to eat or sleep well, so where in this world can they get time to do meditation. Assuming for a moment that few people don't have time, and for those people, instead of not doing meditation at all, they follow some quick exercises that fit into their schedules, while doing other activities.

Below are a few meditation exercises we can easily incorporate into our daily routines.

1. Walking meditation

Breathe slowly and deeply. Stand up straight and feel your feet, legs, back, upper body, neck, and head to create awareness of your whole body. While at it, remember to pay attention to the body movement and repeat.

Walking meditation is a type of technique where you move and adjust your body in a meditative state, thereby creating awareness of your body. Take 10-15 minutes and walk with no purpose but to meditate at least 3 times in a week.

2. Do a mindful body scan

A body scan is a meditative practice in which you focus on each of your body, often beginning at the toes and moving to the head, focusing on the movement and paying attention to how you feel. You can do this while going to your bed--no extra time need be spared for sitting in a pose.

3. Lying in bed

Before you go to sleep, take a moment to think of one thing you were grateful for that happened that day, no matter how big or small, or how difficult the day was. This exercise will help condition your mind for positivity and help you sleep better.

4. Touching your face or body

It might sound bit stupid, but try this out. Gently touch your face, cheeks, and nose and feel the touch. Feel the sensation in your fingers, etc. You'll generate love and compassion for yourself with this technique.

5. Stopping at a red light

Every time you stop at a red light, take a deep breath and try to relax any tension you might be holding in your jaw, neck or shoulders. Take this as an opportunity to relax; after all it's just a matter of few minutes, and you can use them mindfully to observe yourself.

6. When waiting

Whenever you find yourself waiting, whether it be for a meeting, at a bus stop, or before appointment, try to relax all the muscles in your face—your jaw, your brows, and your eyelids.

7. Eating food

Try to remember the last time you ate food and enjoyed each bite. We always eat food like finishing some work, but you can find mindfulness in this activity too. Be mindful. Look at the food, pick up the bite in your hand, watch it, look at the color and texture of the food, smell it. Then put in your mouth and feel the chewing. Then feel the taste and observe the sensation when the food is passing through your throat to your body.

8. Talking to someone

Try to be completely present in the conversation, making eye contact and listening to what they are saying without thinking about what you want to add next or where you're going to be later.

9. Follow an insect

This is real fun. Next time you see an insect, forget everything else around you and watch how it moves for a few seconds. Be aware that it's a living being just like you. Don't label it, just watch it and let the thoughts come and go; you simply become witness to it.

10. Taking off your shoes

When you reach home, don't be in hurry to take off your shoes. Rather, remove the shoes slowly, then remove the socks. Feel the sensation in your feet as they are exposed to a fresh environment. Pay attention to how your feet feel on the ground; try to move your toes around and feel each one individually.

11. Do nothing for 5 minutes

Nothing means nothing. Do nothing for five minutes. Just sit there and be observant of whatever is going on around and inside you. No checking your cell phone or reading a newspaper. If any feelings come up—discomfort, restlessness, boredom or even guilt that you're not doing anything—just embrace them.

"Doing nothing is better than being busy doing nothing."– Lao Tzu

Chapter 4: Mindful Children: A Strong Foundation for Life

Children feel stress and a range of other emotions, both positive and negative, similar to adults; but the difference is that as adults, our minds and bodies have matured enough to use learned coping strategies to bring us back to a centered place that resides in the present, not the past or the future. It is important as a parent or caregiver to be responsible for teaching children how to cope with stress and emotions by demonstrating mindfulness.

According to a child and adolescent psychiatrist at Georgetown University, Jeff Bostic, the essence of mindfulness is tolerating experienced sensations that come into the body, rather than trying to get them to stop immediately.

Often, we teach our children to suppress their feelings by telling them not to get angry or stay quiet, even in the midst of the stressful situation. Instead of teaching them not to react and suppress their feelings, mindfulness practice teaches them to experience all those sensations or emotions arising from an unhealthy environment. Mindfulness doesn't require suppressing feeling; rather, it teaches a way to become aware of them; and this awareness at the deeper level guides us to take the right action in moments of stress or aggression.

How Mindfulness Practice can Benefit Your Child

Research shows that parents and guardians who practice mindfulness around their children contribute to improving their child's sense of self-worth and self-esteem. Practicing mindfulness around your kids will increase their decision-making abilities, as it makes them aware of their environment and calmer.

Studies suggest that teaching meditative practices to children can improve their ability to pay attention, control their tantrums, and make more considered choices.

According to scholars, mindfulness has been found to:

1. Improve mental health and wellbeing
2. Reduce attention problems (according to Crescentini, Capurso, Furlan, & Fabbro, 2016)
3. Improve social skills when well taught and practiced in children and adolescents
4. Mitigate the effects of bullying (Zhou, Liu, Niu, Sun, & Fan, 2016)
5. Enhance focus in children with ADHD (Zhang et al., 2016)

Noted other benefits of mindfulness on children:

1. It helps with the executive function

The executive function is a set of mental skills that comprised of attention, switching focus, planning, organizing and remembering details. Mindfulness practice in school can improve the child in many areas.

In a study conducted on preschoolers, children who went through a mindfulness curriculum for 12 weeks earned higher marks on academic performance measures and showed greater improvements in areas that predict future success (Flook et al., 2015).

2. It helps with social skills

A social skill is any skill we use to interact and communicate with others which can affect listening, understanding, and the classroom climate. Research conducted on lower-income and ethnic minority elementary school children shows that a 5-week mindfulness curriculum can lead to better participation in activities, and caring and respect for others in 9th-grade children (Black et al., 2013).

3. It helps them handle stress better

According to a study by Schonert-Reichl and his colleagues (2010), mindfulness practice leads to higher scores on self-report measures of optimism and positive emotions in elementary school students. Children have a positive and a calmer outlook when they practice stress reduction programs in their homes or schools.

Introducing Mindfulness to your Child

Plato once said that a child's mind is a "tabula rasa", meaning a clean slate. The child forms a fertile soil to plant any good seed. There is no specific age to learn mindfulness; as soon as you notice your child is troubled or stressed, you can start a technique that will help ease him or her. An example is telling the child to sit in a quiet room and think about pleasant things to help calm the mind.

Not every pattern will be good for your child, so you need to study what they like and do something that revolves around it.

Steps to Prepare a Child

1. Practice mindfulness for them to see

Children react to what they see; hence, when they see you doing it, they will follow. Practice it by setting a daily reminder. You know that when you teach another person, you have to be good and established in it, so you know what you're doing.

2. Talk to them

Another way to make children practice mindfulness is by talking to them, asking about their day: what they ate and how it tasted and looked, how they were feeling and what upset them, etc. as this will help calm the child.

3. Create a mindful bedtime ritual

Bedtime is a great time to introduce mindfulness to kids. A full body scan can be done before bed; this is when they close their eyes and pay full attention to their feet, thighs, stomach, arms, and head.

4. Go for a walk

Go for a walk with your child and point to signs and names they may not know or have seen. This will enable them to be more aware of the moment around them.

5. Talk to them about mindfulness

You should let children know what you want to introduce and why they need it. You should explain in plain language the benefits they'd love to hear about. It is important to communicate the concepts and benefits so they know what is happening and understand it better.

Mindfulness Activities for Children

1. Mindful posing

Children watch a lot of cartoons and as mentioned earlier, they learn from what they see, so it is healthy to be familiar with what they see.

There is a lot of fictional superhero comedy in children's TV like Superman, Batman, Wonder woman, etc. Since the kids fancy it, it is nice to start the mindfulness practice from here; you can make them wear costumes and stand head high to let them feel brave, strong and happy.

2. The mindful jar

This activity allows children to take hold of their emotions. It can be done by simply filling a glass jar with water and then pouring in glitters and shaking.

After this is done, you tell the child that this is how the mind works; it can get cloudy, but over time, it cools off like when the glitters finally settles in the jar.

A randomized-controlled study done during the 2011-12 school year demonstrates the social and emotional benefits that occurred over a 6-week time period. Children showed an increase in attention, calmness, social compliance, and caring towards others.

3. Mindfulness walk

This activity helps children become more self-aware of items in their surroundings.

Take them on a walk and tell them to identify or count what they notice on their way. This activity turns an average, everyday walk outside into an exciting new adventure.

4. Blindfolded taste tests

Use a blindfold to cover your child's eye and have him or her experience eating a small piece of food, like a raisin or a cranberry, as if it were their first time eating it. This will help develop their sense of smell and mindfulness.

5. Playing with balloons

Tell your kids that the aim of this game is to keep the balloon off the ground, as they move it slowly and gently. You can tell them to pretend the balloon is very fragile if that helps. This activity helps children increase their focus, as well as their attention span. It might not be the easiest thing to do, but the enjoyment that comes with it does much to compensate for the difficulty.

How do you know your tactic is working?

You know if it is working by observing or asking the child how they feel before, during and after practicing mindful awareness and techniques. You also have to know that the desired result cannot come in just a day or week; so be patient and calm.

A take-home message

Research shows that mindfulness is capable of improving mental health and well-being, attention, self-regulation, and social competency when properly taught and practiced in children and adolescents. However, we need to clearly differentiate the difference between having quiet time and a period of punishment, so they don't think we are trying to impose an act on them.

Introducing mindfulness-based programs in schools and everyday practice can have a life-long impact on the psychological, social, and cognitive well-being of children and teens. So go out and help your child practice and enjoy simple mindfulness exercises when they are young.

Chapter 5: Mindfulness for Adults: Techniques, Fun and Activities

Now that you understand the benefits of mindfulness and are geared up to start doing it, this chapter will enrich you with many techniques, games and activities to instill mindfulness in your daily routine.

When you practice mindfulness regularly, you can achieve your desired result faster because as you become aware of the present moment, you gain access to resources you might not have had before to change your response to some situations. With the help of mindfulness, you become more resourceful and can decide the course of action best suited to your needs. Plus, you significantly improve the quality of your responses with enhanced awareness.

I will now discuss some techniques/ exercises and games that you can explore to have fun as you work towards discovering yourself and your environment.

Mindfulness Techniques/ Exercises

Here are few wonderful mindfulness techniques that can improve awareness and improve the quality of your behavior and actions.

1. The five senses exercise

This is a simple exercise where you use your five senses--sight, smell, sound, taste and touch--to be aware of your surroundings by noticing five things you can see, five things you can smell, five things you can feel, five things you can hear and one thing you can taste at the moment.

This short exercise can be done anywhere at any time, and the main focus is to bring awareness to your current moment in a short amount of time.

2. The self-compassion pause

The self-compassion pause[4] is a mindfulness exercise for those who find it difficult to show compassion to themselves, although they might show it to others. This

---

[4] https://mindfulnessexercises.com/self-compassion-pause/

exercise helps bring awareness to emotions and staying in the moment with them. By taking moments throughout your day to pause and practice self-compassion, you can gradually increase this quality and make it a more regular habit in your life.

Here is how you do it:

- When you find yourself stressed out in a difficult situation, take a moment to pause.
- Reach up and touch your heart, or give yourself a hug if you are comfortable with that.
- Take a few deep breaths.
- Acknowledge that you are suffering and see if you can treat yourself with as much kindness as you would a dear friend or child, who was struggling.
- Offer yourself phrases of compassion, first by acknowledging your suffering:

    - "This is suffering." or "This is really painful/difficult right now" or "Wow, I am really suffering right now!"

- "Suffering is a part of being human."

- For the final phrase(s), choose whatever is most appropriate for your situation. Feel free to use any of the following phrases or create your own:
  - May I hold myself with compassion.
  - May I love and accept myself just as I am.
  - May I experience peace.
  - May I remember to treat myself with love and kindness

This exercise is designed to help us acknowledge that we feel pain and hurt and can love ourselves regardless. The aim of this exercise is to feel compassion for oneself.

3. Breathing

The Three Minute Breathing Space exercise is quick to perform and easy to get started. It is broken into three sections, one per minute. The first minute is for answering questions that have to do with your aspirations, focusing on feelings, thoughts, and sensations. The second minute is spent on keeping awareness of the breath. The last minute is still focusing on your breath, while you try to pay attention to your whole body.

4. Listening

This exercise is designed to open your ears to sounds in a non-judgmental way and to train your mind to be less swayed by the influence of past experiences and preconceptions. Listen intently to music without judging the genre; explore the sound of the instruments and the vocals, and then enjoy it.

5. Mindful immersion

Be mentally involved in the activity of the time. Don't do it because of the desired outcome; do it to feel it, to focus on it, and fully experience it. For example, when you are doing a household chore like washing clothes, feel the texture of the material and notice your actions.

The idea is to get creative and discover new experiences within a familiar routine task.

Mindfulness Games

Have you ever noticed that when you are having fun, time goes by swiftly and you forget your worries and relax? It is often said to go out and play games at least 1-3 times a week because it helps reduce stress.

There are a couple of mindfulness games that are fun. Try them out either as a one-man or group activity. It is best to talk about the reason you are in that space. Especially when in a group, talk about mindfulness, your experience and issues as a form of engagement before you dwell on the fun game without overwhelming anyone.

Some of the games are:

1. Card game

This game can be played in a group or with just two persons. There are various game modes depending on the group playing, but they all incorporate mindfulness, communication, and connection to help people learn and master the practice.

Card games can be played anywhere as they come in a pack that can easily be carried in the pocket for transportation.

2. The M & M game

The M&M Game is an icebreaker that allows people to get to know each other. An M & M is a colorful button-shaped chocolate (with the letter "m" printed in lower case on each candy with vegetable dye); it is used to make the game more fun. There are various techniques, and it can be played in groups or individually. One of the types is the Gratitude Game usually played during Thanksgiving or a family gathering where you write down what you are thankful for. Another one is an anger management type where you write down or say what makes you angry, the choices you've made while angry, and what calmed you.

You can spice up the game by telling jokes in between, but the main goal is to let it out and be calm afterward.

3. Out loud noting

This can be practiced individually or a group. The idea of this game is to aid listening, observation and attention. It can be done by sitting in a circle if possible, noting out loud things you all are thinking, seeing, hearing, or feeling in your bodies. To make this game fun, try and make it simple and do it over and over--like 3 times.

4.   Attentive game

This game can be done by both children and adults to help them focus and be attentive. It can be done in a circle where a participant starts by shouting the name of a popular person or anybody, and the next person has to shout the name of another famous person; this goes around until someone fails and leaves the circle for the rest.

5.   Adult coloring books

Adult coloring books are one of the most interesting anti-stress tools that can unleash creativity and help one focus on a particular task at a time. It is proven to diminish the effects of stress and anxiety. It is also a great guide for beginners who find mindfulness difficult.

6.   Better ME's game of growth

This is a great game for mindful conversations. It is a question game that enables participants to self-reflect and share stories about themselves like their philosophy, achievements, setbacks and goals. The best part of this game is the conversing, as it helps you get to know other participants and do some activities together that you don't regularly do, like writing or gardening.

Mindfulness Activities for Adults

We have exercises and we also have activities that are done in sessions, especially for beginners who are yet to adapt to mindfulness techniques. These sessions can be done in groups or by yourself. Some common mindfulness activities are:

1. Put objects in a paper bag and have each group member put their hand in the bag and try to identify objects. Put the names of the objects on paper with no identifying information; and when everyone has picked, read all the pieces of paper and see how many of the objects were identified correctly.

2. Stand in a circle; pass a small ball of yarn around by unraveling it. Have participants pass it to each other holding the yarn as it unravels, and only passing it to each group member

once. Once everyone is holding onto the yarn, wind it up by passing it around in the opposite order, being careful not to get it tangled or letting it drop.

3. Play Two Truths and a Lie. This is a very common game that can be adapted where each person in the group tells three things about themselves. Then the group members have to guess which one is the lie and why they think their choice is the lie.

4. Play a "P" Past "N" Now "F" Future game. Begin by giving each participant a sheet of paper and a pen, asking them to write down all of their thoughts for 3 minutes after which they label those dealing with the past with the letter "P", those of now with the letter "N", and those of the future with the letter "F". Turn the sheet around and divide it into 3 columns, then they talk about it and tally the thoughts in each one.

Chapter 6: Simple Ways for Everyday Mindfulness

Mindfulness is not like your yearly vacation that you do for 2 weeks and then get back to work. Rather, it's like taking a bath and needs to be done every day. It's like cleansing of your mind, therefore requiring some daily effort.

Mindfulness needs be practiced consistently in our daily lives with an open mind and receptive heart for us to achieve our desired goals and be calm while at it. In this chapter, you will learn various ways to be mindful in your routine life.

Ways to be Mindful

"The basic root of happiness lies in our minds; outer circumstances are nothing more than adverse or favorable."- Matthieu Ricard

We are faced with a lot of responsibilities, targets, deadlines, expectations, and security issues like social, finance, environment, etc.; but we need to remain calm in the storm. It is not easy to stay calm with so much stress around, which is why it becomes more important than ever to practice mindfulness on a regular day-to-day basis. There are ways to practice mindfulness during our crazy schedules:

1.   Do one thing at a time

Do your activities one at a time and take time to focus on it, through it, and observe it. When walking, walk, when eating, eat; don't try to do something alongside.

2.   Take a five-minute break

At least take a break where you don't do anything. Just take 5 minutes to focus on your breathing and notice your environment. There is something called the Pomodoro Technique that is popular for enhancing productivity with the underlying principle that our minds need to take frequent rest as we discharge our routine functions. Under the Pomodoro Technique, you work for a stretch of 25 minutes, then you take a break for 5 minutes. After a total three rounds of this pattern of 25 minutes of work and a five minutes break, you then go for a longer break of fifteen minutes. During each break time, you disengage from your work; maybe you take a brief walk around your workstation. This helps your brain relax and engage in the work afresh after the break. There is an app that helps schedule this work and break structure known as Clockwork Tomato[5], so you can easily apply this technique.

3. Take time to pay attention to others

When you take time to listen to other people, they acknowledge it and may come back to talk things through with you, because they know you will listen and understand. Even if you don't fully understand, they will take because they know you pay attention. This helps to build attention span and the act of mindful listening.

4. Mindful eating

Eating is one of life's pleasure, but we ignore it because we have so many things to do such that we forget food helps us grow and become strong. When you sit to eat, take the time to look at your food--the color and the

_____

[5]
https://play.google.com/store/apps/details?id=net.p hlam.android.clockworktomato&hl=en_GB

aroma—and above all, be fully present in the moment to experience it.

5. Mindful walking

Walking can give you a chance to spend time being mindful without taking extra time from your day. When having a mindful walk around the park or your neighborhood, be aware of your surroundings: the details of the animals running around, the cars, the clothes you are wearing, the way you are striding. Also focus on your breath and be aware of the sensation of standing.

6. Pay full attention to your senses

The essence of mindfulness is to de-clutter the mind and use your senses to achieve inputs. Explore the world, visually seeing your environment and observing or feeling things; but the main focus is to fully engross your mind without judging.

7. Mindful driving

It is not so easy to do while driving, especially when there is traffic. It is possible to zone out because we are tired and frustrated; plus numerous thoughts surface so that we rarely focus purely on the driving itself.

To practice mindful driving, concentrate on your hands, especially during the little turnings, and maintain open awareness by observing the things that pass, like the birds, and the cars beside, behind and in front of you. Lastly, acknowledge openly what arises in your body and mind afterward.

Home Chores that Helps in Mindfulness

In a Florida State University study, half of the participants were primed to be mindful of the dishwashing sensory experience, and the other half were to focus on proper techniques. The outcome was that the mindful dishwashers evidenced a greater state mindfulness, increases in positive affects (i.e., inspiration), decreases in elements of negative affect (i.e., nervousness), and overestimations of dishwashing time.

This means that you can use the time spent doing chores as a mini-meditative session to promote your own mindfulness, while bearing in mind that you need to focus on what you're doing and what it feels like in each moment.

Some common household chores during which to practice mindfulness:

1. Cleaning

Cleaning is one chore not on the top five lists for many. People would rather outsource the task and pay to avoid doing it. Do it without judging and feel the presence.

2. Making your bed

Making your bed every morning sets the pace for you. It makes you want to accomplish what you set out to do that day without rushing into it. You simply take your time to arrange the bed and make it look nice and neat before moving to the next task.

3. Cooking

Enjoy your time in the kitchen; don't try to finish on time. Feel each step of the process and breathe in every aroma. First of all, sit down and breathe, then bring out the ingredients; take time to read the instructions and prepare accordingly.

Visualize and have a theme for the cooking to make it more fun and creative; then admire what you have made and dish it out, indulging in it with all your senses.

4. Organizing your room

This is another household chore that might be a handful, but studies show that clutter is a major source of stress in the home, so the best way to eliminate it is to mindfully tackle it head-on.

The best way to go about this is to attentively place objects where they will be seen as you de-clutter. For instance, place your laptop, jotter, pen and glasses in one corner of your reading table; doing this will make you feel lighter when things are in order.

There are other household chores that can be done as you practice mindfulness such as watering indoor plants, taking care of the garden, feeding pets, washing the car, among others.

Tips for Practicing Mindfulness Everyday

The idea of being mindful is to stay present in the moment and aware of things around you. We are faced with so many activities and responsibilities that we forget to live and enjoy the here and now. Take a minute or two to breathe and meditate; cultivating mindfulness will help you achieve your goals and enjoy life more.

By being mindful, you enjoy everything you are doing: the food you eat, your walk and your chores. To be consistent in practicing mindfulness, there are mindfulness tips to help you understand the process:

1. Focus on developing concentration

Concentration is the constant partner of mindfulness; mindfulness is a great observer-- being aware of things around you and feelings without being distracted or judgmental. It is very difficult to focus on exercising mindfulness when our mind wanders without us noticing; but as you get familiar with the process, you will be able to refocus almost immediately.

2. Sit often

Sitting in meditation is a common exercise practiced in mindfulness, allowing us to focus on our breathing while sitting without being distracted. You can easily get distracted while standing, so this is a preferable practice, especially for beginners.

3. Prioritize mindfulness

When you organize and prioritize your daily activities, it makes it easy to handle them, and the same goes for the practice of mindfulness. You need to prioritize or make a schedule so you do not skip or forget.

When you start a new habit, the mind wanders, and you will likely have excuses to go back to your old ways. So prioritize and stick with your schedule and gradually you will get used to it while you enjoy more.

4. Be patient

Mindfulness takes time and patience to develop; but with practice, you'll notice your ability improve; like everything, the more you practice, the more you get used to it and it becomes easier.

5. Have fun

Most importantly, while practicing, have fun. The main goal of mindfulness is to savor the moment, enjoy it, feel and breathe it. Have fun; you can never get that moment back; and when you enjoy something, your drive to achieve it is high.

Chapter 7: Mindfulness: Challenges & Troubleshooting

Once you start learning and practicing mindfulness, you soon realize the challenges like body aches, restlessness, sleepiness, etc. But here is a different way to look at it: in reality, a problem is only a problem when you perceive it as such. We go through bumps in life, but the way you perceive things is what matters. When you keep dwelling on a problem, you will perceive it that way only. When we change how we respond to the present moment and accept it for what it is, without wanting to change it, then our entire mood instantly changes.

Given the huge list of advantages mindfulness offers, it's worth spending time and effort to inculcate the practice in our everyday life. This chapter highlights the key challenges that people face when incorporating mindfulness in their lives. You will also learn many techniques to troubleshoot those challenges.

Mindfulness Challenges

How hard can it be to sit still and do nothing at all? Well, mindfulness is not only that, it is also training the mind to be mentally prepared, increasing concentration. The training requires time, effort and commitment to gain the desired outcome. Moreover, being able to overcome the obstacles that come your way from practicing mindfulness actually helps the mind become more focused and resilient to external and internal influences in the process.

Below are some of the challenges of mindfulness.

1. Restlessness

Staying still is a problem for some people; they find themselves getting bored or uncomfortable. To assist, you can try and walk instead of sitting to move your body; you can also try other techniques such as yoga or tai chi.

2. Idleness

Let's face it, when we think about being still for 15 minutes at work, our employers will not take it likely as they see you as

72

unproductive and not willing to work; but according research, the regular practice of mindfulness will boost work performance.

According to Daniel Goleman, attention skills are important for excelling at work because focus is useful for sticking with problems, navigating relationships with colleagues, understanding your own motivations, avoiding emotional reactivity, and fostering innovation.

3. Distractions

Distraction is a natural part of mindfulness meditation; it can certainly be irritating, but it provides an opportunity to observe feelings and acknowledge the fact that it is there. You will notice it and then guide your attention back to what you are focusing on. It is essential that we know these distractions and frustrations will always be there: we need to focus on coping or leaning into them, instead of reacting or running away.

4. Fear

Fear of failure is the major cause of things not getting done, and the fact is we want certainty before starting out. There is no right or wrong in the practice of mindfulness; it is simply accepting one's environment without judging, leaving no room for remarks. You can do it in 5 or 20 minutes as long as you're comfortable. There is no special schedule, and the aim is to enjoy the moment.

5. We do it alone

When we are alone, we tend to think, plan, worry, and predict how things will turn out in future. Basically, this is how the brain is wired; it loves to seek certainty. This is why there are classes, or a group of people gathering around to practice mindfulness. It is not compulsory to be in a group, but it gets us more exposure and we become more social, doing things with others' help. You can read online or in books to understand the techniques and converse with like-minded people.

Troubleshooting Mindfulness Challenges

Here are few tips that can help you overcome those initial challenges that you face during your mindfulness practice.

1. Acceptance

Mindfulness requires acceptance by being non-judgmental at that moment, and to be willing to shake off the negative thoughts and feelings that overwhelm us.

It is hard not to let our minds wander all the time, and it is also hard not to have perceptions about things; but to practice mindfulness, you need to accept the moment and manage it.

2. Determination

Mindfulness takes a lot of work, so do things that make for a beautiful outcome. Thus, you need to work to achieve the desired outcome for yourself; and as much as it may be difficult at first, the longer you practice, the easier it becomes and the more joyful your life.

3. Set a goal

The truth is that when you have a goal in mind, it makes it easier to want to get up and put in the work. As much as it is good to have an objective, don't be too strict about it as this makes it difficult for you to enjoy the activity and have fun. Some good advice is to set a realistic goal and then follow through to achieve it. There is no use in setting high-level goals and then burning yourself out to achieve them.

Don't let your goal frustrate you or make you tense; enjoy the moment and the actions around you and be happy.

4. It lets you care of yourself

Mindfulness gives us the avenue to be in our own space and understand our needs by listening to our bodies and minds, and knowing what they need. Therefore, have faith that everything will be taken care of if you just keep putting in the effort to develop mindfulness.

5. New perspective

The practice of mindfulness allows you to take a step back from your current situation and view things without making erratic judgments. This gives you new insight and lets you view things from another angle, allowing you to find the positives in a seemingly dark place.

How Do You Practice Mindfulness When You Are Overwhelmed?

"Mindfulness is about love and loving life. When you cultivate this love, it gives you clarity and compassion for life, and your actions happen in accordance with that".- Jon Kabat-Zinn

Practicing mindfulness has a lot of advantages and benefits such as increased focus, which gives us the ability to finish what we started almost all the time and connect with ourselves. When overwhelmed, it is blissful to practice mindfulness, as it can release you from the constraints of your physical body without having to go anywhere.

To reduce tension, do one thing at a time, since multitasking slows down your pace. Prioritize tasks to make it easier to get your work done and enjoy small moments because you only live once. Wash away stress by practicing mindfulness and relaxation.

Naturally, we get tense and anxious about what may happen, which is a cause of being overwhelmed in mind and body; but when you trust yourself to handle situations, you become more confident to take on future tasks.

Lastly, mindfulness can be practiced anywhere and at any time, so you don't need to give yourself that much room and be worried about it. It can even be practiced on your way to work or in the toilet, or while walking to the cafeteria.

Balancing Your Life and Mindfulness

It is not so easy trying to get your life together. At work, you're thinking about what to cook at home, the toilet you didn't wash, the floor you didn't mop; and at work you're thinking of accomplishing tasks and what you need to do to get them done before the deadline. All these mixed thoughts overwhelm our bodies and minds; that is when the practice of mindfulness comes in to help us be present in the moment.

According to the World Health Organization, the cost of stress to American business is as high as $300 billion, an estimate that includes healthcare and lost productivity because of diabetes, high blood pressure, and other illnesses. For most businesses, stress reduction and mindfulness have become a key part of wellness efforts.

Even a small practice of mindfulness in your day can help you lead a life of balance and self-care, improving both your well-being and work-related efforts.

- Pay attention to your body's need

Pay attention to your body; feed it what it deserves, so it wouldn't conk out. Does it want 5 minutes of relaxation from the stress of work? So give them by going out for a walk and fresh air. When you listen to your body and give it what it wants, you'll find your focus and concentration levels benefit. Learn to listen to your body and take care of it.

- Be calm

When you make the choice to be calm, you begin to enjoy life. Our flight-fight reflex mode is there, where we unconsciously want to flee from a scene or be confrontational, but the ability to control the mind before it gets to that state is what makes you mindful. Move away from the scenario that wants you to be tense. Go for a walk or better yet try the breathing technique.

- Focus on the job at hand

There are distractions around us, some important, some not so much; the ability to focus and finish up the task at hand is the aim without giving much thoughts to the others. It is faster and easier. Also, don't procrastinate unless it is not urgent or difficult and has to be done in bits.

- Meditation and breathing exercises

These are common exercises in mindfulness that can be done anywhere and very easily, although we have others. Do not forget to meditate to bring the body and mind together and relax as well as breathe in and out to get rid of negative energy and calm the senses.

- Focus on the present

When you're in the office, then be in the office; and when you're at home, be at home. This makes it easier to get things done. Also, don't forget to interact with your colleagues at work which can help get your attention off the overwhelming workload. It also helps you build interpersonal skills, which is good for you as well as the organization. Outside the workplace, make friends and be with them to enrich your experience. Live in the moment and enjoy!

Chapter 8: Enrich Your Workplace Through Mindfulness

It is a known fact backed up by researches that mindfulness impacts a person positively if practiced regularly; and the benefits can also be seen in the workplace. It improves productivity and creativity, and eventually there is growth for all. Many employers such as Google, Target, Nike, Apple and Yahoo, among others, have taken it upon themselves to integrate and create programs in the workplace to help employees take part in mindfulness and promote self-care.

Recent training industry research, conducted by Allen Communication, found that 88 percent of respondents believe that relevant and consistent training content makes learning and development more palatable. 73 percent believe that communications need to stand out more. A study conducted at the University of Washington also found that those who had meditation training in the workplace were able to stay on task longer and were less distracted, as meditation improves memory and alleviates stress.

Creating Programs in the Workplace

Before you implement any mindfulness training program, make sure the training fits with your organizational culture. If the benefits don't align with the employee's everyday work and the organization's goal, it definitely will not work long term, so do some research and find ways to incorporate the programs like:

1. Hire a mindfulness expert

Hire a mindfulness expert or ask an employee who already practices mindfulness to take a workshop session on certain days to teach others, going from meditation to yoga to tai chi to the breathing technique. Do not make it a compulsory requirement because it then deflects from the aim of meditation which is to be aware of and accept your thoughts and feelings. It may not happen if a person is forced.

2. Retreat

Find a place in the office like a backspace and create a designated room where people can go to practice mindfulness games or other recreational activities that might help them relax and enjoy. This will help refresh the employees and give them a break from work activities to calm their minds before going back to the task.

3. Mindfulness sessions

Create a mindfulness session, which can be 30 minutes a day, to revitalize employees. In this session, employees can go out for mindful walks, do mindful breathing, and meditate to calm their nerves. The time should be set when there is less work because employees are tired.

4. Feedback

In the recent workplace culture, people get motivated by just being praised for their work and by being told they did great in a project. Positive feedback goes a long way to help the practice of mindfulness in the workplace; so give positive feedback and award employees who display qualities of mindfulness in their everyday work and watch them take it to heart.

5. Interpersonal relationships

In Adam's Maslow hierarchy, the social stage is where there is need to connect with others, the need for friends, and for a relationship. It is paramount and can help mindfulness when you interact with others. It also helps interpersonal relationships in the workplace as well as productivity when people can accommodate themselves and help each other do their work. In effect, they create a healthy working environment. It also makes room for empathy as you listen to others and put yourself in the next person's shoes, understanding his or her reaction to a task or why he/she responded in a certain way.

How to Incorporate Mindfulness into Your Workday

1. Take a minute or two after you wake up to take a deep breath and focus on the present. When we wake up, we release the most stress hormones of the day, so take time out to be mindful before you jump into the day's tasks.

2. When you arrive at the office after all that traffic, pause to relax and take a deep breath or do the Three Minute Breathing Space before you continue your day. It stabilizes your nerves and provides a good rhythm to kick off the day's work.

3. During the day, avoid multitasking. A lot of companies will tell you that when you multitask, efficiency drops up to 40 percent. Doing one thing at a time is easier and shorter, allowing you to finish the whole activity even faster than if you were multitasking.

4. Take a break, find a place to digest, and be present in the moment. It can be in the toilet, cafeteria, or when talking to colleagues. Enjoy the moment and banish all thoughts of work for those few minutes, and you'll return to your desk feeling refreshed and refocused.

5. On your way home, try to de-stress by focusing on your breath and allowing yourself to relax and recharge. Instead of playing with

your phone or listening to music, try and do something new.

Try these steps at least 2-3 times a week and write down how you feel and what you noticed afterward; you will then see a great impact and improvement in your mind, body, and soul.

Ways to Be More Mindful at Work

Our mind wanders consistently and it can make us overwhelmed; which is why it is helpful to practice mindfulness in the workplace to help us relax and calm our thoughts and feelings. When you have a whole load of work to do, you may want to ignore going on a break, but this actually helps calm your mind and make you more focused.

Research shows that people spend almost 47 percent of their waking hours thinking about something other than what they're doing. In other words, many of us operate on autopilot, making the ability to maintain focus and concentration very important.

Below are some ways to be more mindful at work:

1. Be present

When you're consciously present at work, you are aware of what's going on around you. Repel the clouds of absentmindedness. Give your full attention and focus on a task, and when your mind wanders, acknowledge it and get back on track. Do not be easily carried away.

2. Mindful exercises

Practice some mindfulness exercises find peace of mind, heal stress, improve brain function, boost mood, and live in the moment. Mindful breathing, mindful walking, mindful eating, and maybe yoga, are some of the exercises you can practice: a 15-minute break can be taken to rebalance your nervous system and tone down the fight-or-flight response.

3. Mindful reminders

It is easy to forget when you have so much going on in your head, and the brain's normal (default) mode is to be habitually getting lost in your own thoughts.

Research undertaken at Harvard University shows that 47 percent of a person's day can be spent lost in thoughts, which can have a negative impact on well-being. You have about 85 thousand seconds in a day, and it is in your best interest not to waste any one irresponsibly. By wandering in the sea of unguided thoughts, you are not being responsible enough for your time.

You can use some types of reminders to help you recall the task you need to do such as setting an alarm, writing down a note, setting an appointment on your phone, calendar or sticky note, or using bells.

4. Feel gratitude

We focus more on the bad than the good, which is why we read blogs, news and criticize the negative comments about someone. This is bad, but we are wired to think this way: humans have a negativity bias.

However, we can try and focus on the good of others by being positive. Start by writing a positive comment to someone on Twitter or tell the colleague next to you that you like her dress or shoes. Buy lunch for a junior staff member because of the effort he put in the task you asked him to do. This form of appreciation motivates the other party; empirical pieces of evidence support this.

Plenty of evidence suggests that actively practicing gratitude makes you feel better and has a positive impact on creativity, health, working relationships, and one's quality of work.

5. Put your phone down

Our phone is our life; without it we feel empty, especially in this digital and fast-paced life where we go to the Internet for every breaking piece news and read tons of information on our portable devices. In fact, one study reveals that workers are 26 percent more productive when they're not attached to their phones. If you want to accomplish a task on time, you need to put that phone down and out of sight. If you have to touch your phone, you can give yourself digital breaks.

6. Take a break

The body needs food. Don't play with it; this is why we are given at least an hour lunch break at work to eat, walk, and relax.

According to research from the University of Illinois at Urbana-Champaign, brief breaks actually significantly improve focus, and better yet, paying attention to what you're eating may even reduce overall caloric intake.

7. Mindfulness in office meetings

If you work in an environment where you are required to have a lot of meetings with other colleagues in the organization, you probably know that they can be a big drain on your energy and productivity. They are often not even relevant to your most pressing work priorities or long-term goals. As economist John Kenneth Galbraith once said, "Meetings are indispensable when you don't want to do anything." According to a 3M meeting network survey of executives, 25 to 50% of the time people spend in meetings is wasted.

This said, meetings still can be a great time to reconnect with peers and practice a beginner's mind-set as you address challenges, generate ideas, and look for solutions. Rather than thinking of meetings as a waste of time, you can practice mindfulness before and during these sessions to make them more valuable to you and other attendees.

Here is what you should do: before entering the meeting, be mindful of your emotions.

Maybe you are happy, overwhelmed, angry, stressed, or whatever--just be mindful. This will help you understand how you perceive the nature of that meeting, i.e., do you look forward to it or want to avoid it. Whatever the feeling is, just embrace it--embracing the feeling itself is an act of mindfulness. Now when you have entered the meeting, be totally present and stay focused on the topic at hand. Don't be afraid and put across your point. Keep watching your emotions before you speak during the meeting. Is it fear, stress, anxiety, or what? Notice each emotion and feeling. This way, you can turn your seemingly unproductive meeting into mindfulness practice.

8. Clear your workstation

The place you work at everyday needs to be clear of unnecessary objects and things. If you see things cluttered around, it can be distracting and often irritates. Clutter loosens your focus and becomes a dent in your productivity. Moreover, others around you get a message that you are disorganized and scattered.

You can find your own piece of mindfulness meditation in cleaning your workstation.

Remove the extra papers, the bunch of pens and pencils, and keep them in their dedicated place on your desk. While cleaning the desk, don't simply treat this as a mundane activity; rather do it with full attention and engagement. Throw the unnecessary material in the trash. Cleaning the work area in a focused manner is in itself an act of mindfulness practice – while clearing the desk with full focus on the work, you clean your mind as well. Once your desk is clear, you have set the stage for more mental and emotional energy, and the necessary focus to begin your work.

Tips for Practicing Mindfulness at Work

We are so engrossed with work that we forget to live. We are either checking work emails or doing a project for an amazing future; that's fine, but at the end of the day, do you see what you're doing or just do it without giving it a second thought? Our tendency to cruise along on auto-pilot limits creativity and makes us less productive, while it strains relationships.

We practice mindfulness to remember to live in the moment and be aware of our surroundings. This helps improve productivity and relax our minds and bodies.

1. Notice the way your body reacts

Have you tried to notice the way your body reacts after you leave a meeting that didn't go so well? What do you do to relax, or do you notice how your body reacts when you meet your target or get praised? Does your heart race and how do you relax your muscles? Take time out to notice these things, as simply being aware of your physical responses can help you make small daily adjustments.

This practice will help you know what to do to relax your muscles and feel more in control when you anticipate your response to some situations.

2. Pause for a moment

Before you start your work for the day, take a moment to pause and observe. Pay attention to your surroundings, especially the little things you usually ignore. This might seem very unworthy, but it is a mindful reflection that can help you break out of old ways and allow you refocus. No need for too much rush; after all, they say that no matter how fast you live life, you will never be in time to make it out alive. So chill and catch sight of special moments.

3. Practice nonjudgmental observation of others

It is human to want to criticize and make judgments of situations before we hear the full story. However, it is better to be more observant and listen a bit more. Professor and writer, Jon Kabat-Zinn, suggests beginning with nonjudgmental observation: watching and listening closely, but holding back your inner critic, at least at first.

Non-judgmental observation allows you to discover new things about your co-workers and your environment. It is hard, but a little bit of patience is worth it and is an effective way to switch off your internal auto-pilot.

4. Acceptance

To move forward, you need to be able to accept your past. Thinking of the past and what could have or should have been will only hurt; it wouldn't make your present or future any better.

Learn from it and move on, so you can approach similar situations better and with a different perspective next time. If you keep dwelling on the past, it will give you little or no time to focus on the situation at hand, nor prepare for it and give it your best shot.

5. Practice nonjudgmental observation of yourself

The more you train your mind to immediately find fault in your daily actions, the more you'll develop self-doubt and increase your level of stress. Psychologist, Rick Hanson, notes that people have a tendency to learn more from negative experiences, while not learning enough from positive ones.

Stop analyzing your bad decisions and focus on observing more to get things right. The more you beat yourself up for the bad result you might have had, the more you train your mind to be in self-doubt and lose confidence in yourself.

Chapter 9: Mindfulness Based Stress Reduction (MBSR) and Cognitive Therapy (MBCT)

Overcome Stress and Depression with Mindfulness-Based Therapies

Not everyone is the same. Each human being has a different background, lifestyle, personal circumstances and unique past. While some people have the stamina to try out new things and bring change into their lives, others due to a traumatic past or other major disturbances in life find it very difficult to cope up with stress and anxiety. In such cases, people sometimes lose willpower and determination to work on putting their lives back on track. Staying longer in such situations is not advisable, as it only worsens the outcome. Therefore, there arises a need for outside help to handle the situation better.

Realizing this, Jon Kabat-Zinn invented mindfulness-based programs in 1979 and created the Stress Reduction Clinic and the Center for Mindfulness in Medicine, Health

Care, and Society at the University of Massachusetts Medical School. This program known as the Mindfulness Based Stress Reduction (MBSR) Program is now conducted widely across the world. As described earlier, Kabat-Zinn studied the practices of mindfulness and meditations from Buddhist teachers such as Thich Nhat Hanh. His practice of yoga and studies led him to integrate their teachings with scientific findings. As a result, MBSR uses yoga, body awareness, and mindfulness meditation to help people become more mindful.

MBSR program is an 8-week program conducted physically and online. If someone wishes to expedite the process, they can opt for a 5-day residential program at different location organized by the Center for Mindfulness.

MBSR is a structured group program that employs mindfulness meditation to alleviate suffering associated with physical, psychosomatic and psychiatric disorders. The program, both nonreligious and non-esoteric, is based on a systematic procedure to develop and enhance awareness of the moment-to-moment experience of perceptible mental processes.[6]

A recent study[7] published in Social Cognitive and Affective Neuroscience (SCAN) reports that practicing Mindfulness Based Stress Reduction (MBSR) therapy can actually lead to structural changes in the amygdala. This finding is of particular significance because the amygdala has been identified in neurobiological studies as a brain structure that plays a crucial role in stress responses.

In this study, individuals who were stressed but otherwise healthy participated in an eight-week program of MBSR. At the end of the program, each participant reported a significant decrease in perceived stress, as compared to before treatment. MR images of each participant's brain were obtained both before and after the MBSR program. The images show a decrease in the density of the amygdala gray matter after the program, when the participants reported feeling less stress. This is the first study to

[6] https://www.ncbi.nlm.nih.gov/pubmed/15256293
[7] https://academic.oup.com/scan/article/5/1/11/1728269

draw a link between physical, neuroplastic changes and alterations in the one's psychological state.

Research has shown that mindfulness-based stress reduction has helped people with chronic diseases. Participation in an MBSR program is likely to result in coping better with symptoms, improved overall well-being and quality of life, and enhanced health outcomes.[8]

There is another set mindfulness-based programs known as Mindfulness-Based Cognitive Therapy. Per the website of the Center for Mindfulness[9], Mindfulness-Based Cognitive Therapy (MBCT) is an established program to help people prone to recurrent depression.

MBCT combines the practice and clinical application of mindfulness meditation with the tools of cognitive therapy to break the cycle of recurrent depression. It is based on the research of Drs. Zindel Segal, John Teasdale and Mark Williams, and is documented in their book, *Mindfulness-*

---

[8] https://www.ncbi.nlm.nih.gov/pubmed/20815988
[9] https://www.umassmed.edu/cfm/mindfulness-based-programs/mbct-courses/about-mbct/

Based Cognitive Therapy for Depression, a New Approach to Preventing Relapse. MBCT was developed for people with recurring episodes of depression or unhappiness to prevent relapse. It has been proven effective in patients with major depressive disorder who have experienced at least three episodes. MBCT has been shown to improve symptoms of depression in some people with physical health conditions, such as vascular disease and traumatic brain injury.

It is group therapy with once-a-week, two-hour sessions, led by your therapist as part of an eight-week program. You will learn meditation techniques as well as basic principles of cognition, such as the relationship between the way you think and feel. You will have the opportunity to learn more about your depressive condition. MBCT therapists teach patients how to break away from negative thought patterns that can cause a downward spiral into a depressed state, so they will be able to fight off depression before it takes hold.

The Center for Mindfulness also conducts the MBCT program, realizing that people who suffering from depression could get benefitted from this. Since it is based on mindfulness only, it expands the mission of the CFM to offer an evidence-based program designed specifically for those struggling with depression. Per CFM, it offers participants an opportunity to learn a new way of relating to unwanted thoughts and feelings and he powerful skills to respond in an intentional and skilful manner. Participants report feeling a sense of freedom from the trap of emotional suffering that may have been present for many years. While people with a history of depression can benefit from MBSR, MBCT is specifically designed to reveal how depression operates and provide specific tools for this condition. For more details, visit the website of Center for Mindfulness at https://www.umassmed.edu/cfm.

Conclusion

Whatever the origin of mindfulness may be, now it has spread across the world to all areas. Little wonder that mindfulness programs are being incorporated in schools and at the workplaces to boost the cognitive well-being of children and adults.

You already know by now that mindfulness practices have the stamp of scientific evidence for removing stress, anxiety, depression and many other body ailments. You also understand fully the benefits of mindfulness for improving productivity, focus, and creativity by physically altering the size of the brain. The amount of research conducted on the benefits of mindfulness is voluminous.

The best part is that you don't need a great amount of time to start - just 10 minutes to begin. Nor you need to bother about any specific place or body pose. Simply put, knowing the benefits, and comparing the efforts involved, there isn't a single excuse not to start your mindfulness practice today.

The best books in the world can't give you results, if don't put in the effort to implement the message. Even a few wisdom nuggets if implemented well have the potential to transform your life. The choice is entirely yours. Will you keep this book like any other and forget it or try one or two techniques and put mindfulness to use? I hope you'll go the latter route.

That said, I wish you a mindful life full of peace, joy and wisdom.

References

- Definitions of Mindfulness by Linehan, 2015, Wikipedia, Mindful.org, Mayo Clinic and Mindful Awareness Research Center at the University of California at Los Angeles.
- A research by Daniel Stern, a 2012 UCLA, Black (2010)
- History of Mindfulness by Trousselard et al., 2014 in Buddihism, Kabat-Zinn (2013) in US
- Mindfulness curriculum in Virginia Military Institute by Holly Richardson and Matt Jarman
- Quote. Mindfulness Quotes – BrainyQuote
- Mindfulness in Different Buddhist Traditions. Bhikkhu Anālayo, 2016
- History of Mindfulness: From East to West and From Religion to Science. Joaquín, 2017
- 8 Basic Characteristics of Mindfulness. Laura Chang, 2012
- Mindfulness in plain English. Gunaratana B.H., 1996

- The Mind and Mental Health: How Stress Affects the Brain. Rebecca Bernstein, 2016
- 50 Mindfulness Quotes to Inspire - Live Bold and Bloom
- Kocovski, Fleming, Hawley, Huta, & Antony, 2013. 22 Mindfulness Exercises, Techniques & Activities for Adults
- Zhang et al., 2016. Mindfulness Activities for Children and Teens: 25 Fun Exercises For Kids
- 6 Mindfulness Exercises You Can Try Today
- Richard N. Fogoros, MD, 2017. The Health Benefits of Mindfulness-Based Stress Reduction
- Daphne M. Davis, PhD, and Jeffrey A. Hayes, PhD., 2012. What are the benefits of mindfulness?
- Donald, Atkins, Parker, Christie, & Ryan, 2016. The 23 Amazing Health Benefits of Mindfulness for Body and Brain
- Shapiro, S. and Carlson L., (2010). The Art and Science of Mindfulness. Washington DC: American Psychological Association.

- How to Practice Mindfulness (The Ultimate Guide to Being More Mindful Throughout the Day)
- mindful.org, 2011. Getting Started with Mindfulness
- Toni Bernhard J.D., 2014. 7 Myths and Misconceptions about Mindfulness
- AETNA, 2016. 6 Myths about Mindfulness We All Need to Stop Believing
- The Life Blog, 2015. A Brief History of Mindfulness
- Meditation Troubleshooting Guide. Positive Psychology Program, 2017
- Wikipedia. Mindfulness
- Headspace.com, 2013. 5 Ways to Bring Mindfulness into Everyday Life
- Margarita Tartakovsky, M.S., 2012. 7 Easy Ways to be Mindful Every Day
- Karen Kissel Wegela Ph.D., 2010. How to Practice Mindfulness Meditation
- Jon Henley, 2014. Mindfulness: a beginner's guide
- Zheng Wang 2000. Mindfulness at Work for Dummies by Alidina and Adams.

- American Journal of Occupational Therapy 2005. 20 Best Ways to Be More Mindful at Work
- Jon Kabat-Zinn. 7 tips for practicing mindfulness at work
- 10 Big Companies That Promote Employee Meditation. Sonorrari.com, 2017

DISCLAIMER

The author makes no representations or warranties with respect to the accuracy or completeness of the contents of this work and specifically disclaims all warranties, including without limitation warranties of fitness for a particular purpose. No warranty may be created or extended by sales or promotional materials. The advice and recipes contained herein may not be suitable for everyone. This work is sold with the understanding that the author is not engaged in rendering medical, legal or other professional advice or services.

If professional assistance is required, the services of a competent professional person should be sought. The author shall not be liable for damages arising here from. The fact that an individual, organization of website is referred to in this work as a citation and/or potential source of further information does not mean that the author endorses the information the individual, organization to website may provide or recommendations they/it may make. Further, readers should be aware that Internet websites listed in this work might have changed or disappeared between since this work was written and when it is read.

Adherence to all applicable laws and regulations, including international, federal, state, and local governing professional licensing, business practices, advertising, and all other aspects of doing business in any jurisdiction in the world is the sole responsibility of the purchaser or reader.

Made in the USA
Middletown, DE
31 July 2018